2ND EDITION

POP CLASSICS FOR
FINGERSTYLE GUITAR

By CHARLES DUNCAN

ISBN 978-1-5400 9363-9

Visit Hal Leonard Online at
www.halleonard.com

Contact us:
Hal Leonard
7777 West Bluemound Road
Milwaukee, WI 53213
Email: info@halleonard.com

In Europe, contact:
Hal Leonard Europe Limited
42 Wigmore Street
Marylebone, London, W1U 2RN
Email: info@halleonardeurope.com

In Australia, contact:
Hal Leonard Australia Pty. Ltd.
4 Lentara Court
Cheltenham, Victoria, 3192 Australia
Email: info@halleonard.com.au

Introduction to Hal Leonard Pop Classics

This new edition of Fingerstyle Pop Classics updates the original publication in several ways.
(1) It's 16 pages longer, contains nine new hit songs from the 60s through the 80s, and the original arrangements have been enhanced. (2) A few songs which were dated have been deleted to make space for the new, and now all-duet material, (3) Because of the amazing upward progress in the level of playing during the past generation, the new pieces and arrangements are more challenging, and therefore more interesting. (4) They now also provide an introduction to syncopation, which is an important feature of modern music and all styles of guitar playing.

The order of pieces is generally progressive and the syncopation in some of the earlier pieces has been slightly simplified in order to provide an easier entry point. Most of the Broadway hits contain very little, but are fun to play as well as good practice in sight reading and duet playing.

Common forms of Syncopation

The simplest form of syncopation occurs when the strong notes fall on a weak beat, as in the first piece—"All My Loving" by the Beatles. Here, you'll see that when the half notes fall on the second beat, they still get the accent instead of the quarter notes on the first beat.

Probably the most typical kind of syncopation in all forms of pop music puts the accent on the "and" of a divided beat which is then tied to the next beat. Here's a fun example—the first four bars of "Mary Had a Little Lamb" written with a fair amount of syncopation:

Syncopation often falls on the last beat of a measure, with the eighth note tied over the bar line as shown below. It's a quote from the third piece, George Gershwin's "Summertime" (measures 7-9). This typical device anticipates the sound of the downbeat by a fraction to make it more interesting rhythmically and keep it from sounding "square." Count aloud as shown:

The music quote below is the first phrase of "Light My Fire" by The Doors, which is repeated several times throughout the song. It makes a great syncopation exercise if you play it slow and count aloud as shown. Be sure to play decisively on the "ands," sustain the tied notes for full value, and using your metronome, gradually speed it up until it begins to sound and feel right.

A closely related device is the use of quarter note triplets in 4/4 time—you'll see it in a few pieces here. Although technically not syncopation, it's rhythmically tricky in a similar way. The secret is to count the same way you'd count the rhythm in 2/4 as two eighth-notes and an eighth-note triplet except with doubled note values: "one—and two-trip-let, one—and two-triplet," etc. In other words, count it in half-notes as indicated here by the cut time (alla breve) time signature. Use this count in the exercise below to make the 4/4 measures sound just like the 2/4 measures.

Improvising on the repeats

Authentic jazz improvisation takes serious study and several fine Hal Leonard books cover the topic thoroughly—for example, The Hal Leonard Jazz Guitar Method by Jeff Schroedl and The Guitarist's Guide to Scales over Chords by Chad Johnson. However, a good way to get started is to take some liberties with the melody and rhythm on repeats as shown below for "Summertime"— just one of many ways to vary it without losing track of the original melody. Not all the songs in this book are suitable for this kind of variation but you might try it on "Light My Fire," "A Day in the Life of a Fool," "Feelings," or "Yesterday," Experiment with it for fun and keep it simple—just a few tasteful melodic and rhythmic "tweaks" can create a pleasing variety on repeats.

All My Loving

Words and Music by John Lennon and Paul McCartney

Try to Remember

from THE FANTASTICKS
Words by Tom Jones
Music by Harvey Schmidt

To Coda ⊕

D.C. al Coda
(take repeat)

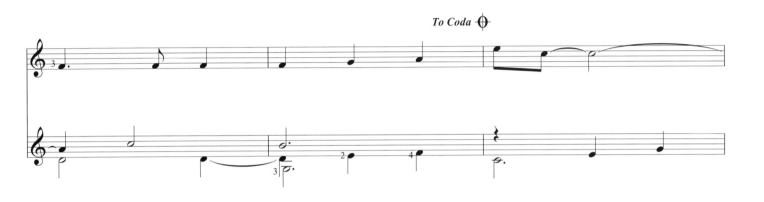

⊕ Coda

molto rit.

molto rit.

Summertime
from PORGY AND BESS®

Music and Lyrics by George Gershwin, DuBose and Dorothy Heyward and Ira Gershwin

Me and Bobby McGee

Words and Music by Kris Kristofferson and Fred Foster

Chim Chim Cher-ee

from MARY POPPINS

Words and Music by Richard M. Sherman and Robert B. Sherman

To Coda ⊕

D.S. al Coda

⊕ **Coda**

13

Do-Re-Mi

from THE SOUND OF MUSIC
Lyrics by Oscar Hammerstein II
Music by Richard Rodgers

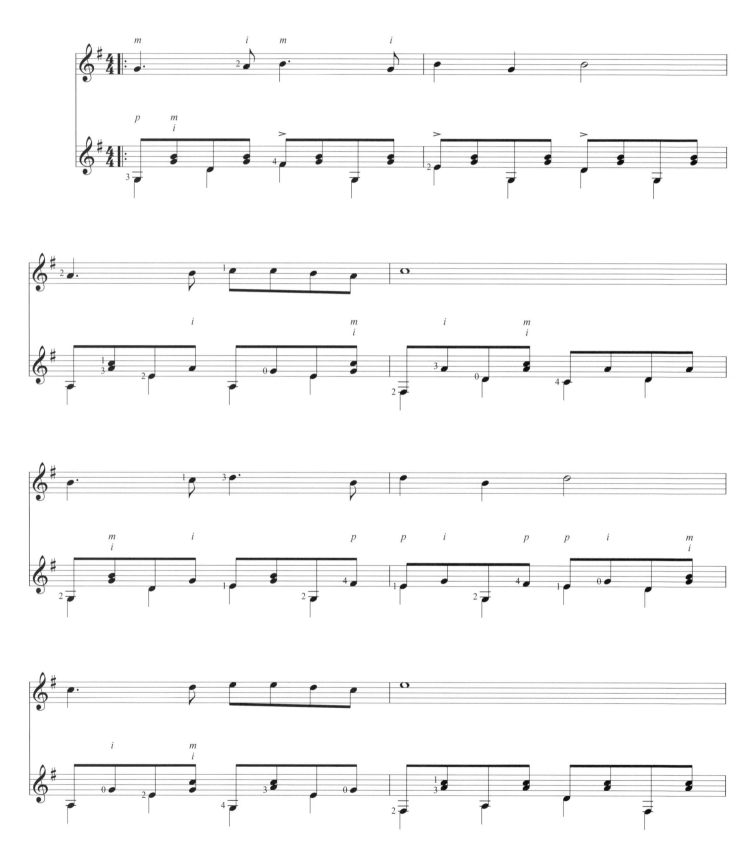

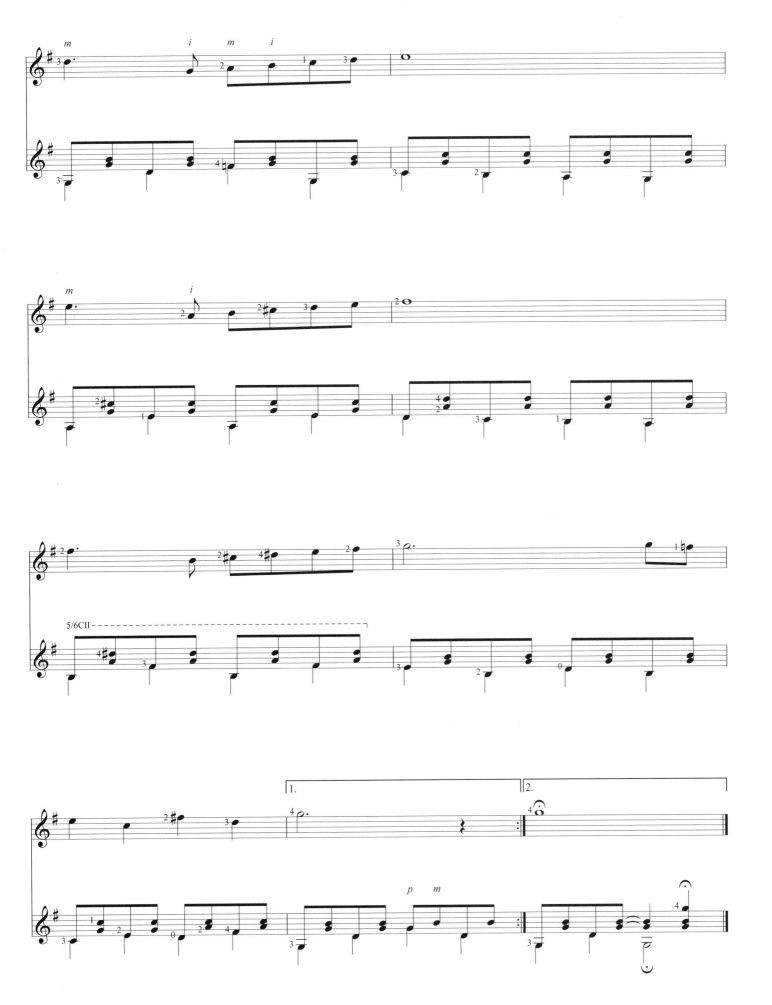

Light My Fire

Words and Music by John Densmore, Robby Krieger, Ray Manzarek and Jim Morrison

Yesterday

Words and Music by John Lennon and Paul McCartney

When I Need You

Words and Music by Carole Bayer Sager and Albert Hammond

To Coda ⊕

D.S. al Coda
(take 2nd ending)

⊕ **Coda**

Get Me to the Church on Time

from MY FAIR LADY

Words by Alan Jay Lerner
Music by Frederick Loewe

23

Time in a Bottle

Words and Music by Jim Croce

To Coda ⊕

D.S. al Coda
(take 2nd ending)

poco rit.

poco rit.

⊕ **Coda**

Play 3 times

Here, There and Everywhere

Words and Music by John Lennon and Paul McCartney

3rd time, To Coda

D.S. al Coda

Coda

It's Too Late

Words and Music by Carole King and Toni Stern

Memory

from CATS

Music by Andrew Lloyd Webber
Text by Trevor Nunn after T.S. Eliot

D.S. al Coda

⊕ **Coda**

rall.

rall.

You're So Vain

Words and Music by Carly Simon

A Day in the Life of a Fool
(Manha De Carnaval)
By Luiz Bonfa

Both Sides Now

Words and Music by Joni Mitchell

To Coda ⊕

D.S. al Coda
(take 2nd ending)

⊕ Coda

2nd time, molto rall.

2nd time, molto rall.

Feelings
(¿Dime?)

English Words and Music by Morris Albert and Louis Gaste
Spanish Words by Thomas Fundora

Come Down in Time

Words and Music by Elton John and Bernie Taupin

D.S. al Coda   ⊕ **Coda**

Freely

Killing Me Softly with His Song

Words by Norman Gimbel
Music by Charles Fox

To Coda ✛

D.S. al Coda

✛ Coda

molto rit.

molto rit.

Meditation
(Meditãcao)

Music by Antonio Carlos Jobim
Original Words by Newton Mendonça
English Words by Norman Gimbel

One Note Samba
(Samba de Uma Nota So)

Original Lyrics by Newton Mendonça
English Lyrics by Antonio Carlos Jobim
Music by Antonio Carlos Jobim

FINGERPICKING GUITAR BOOKS

Hone your fingerpicking skills with these great songbooks featuring solo guitar arrangements in standard notation and tablature. The arrangements in these books are carefully written for intermediate-level guitarists. Each song combines melody and harmony in one superb guitar fingerpicking arrangement. Each book also includes an introduction to basic fingerstyle guitar.

FINGERPICKING ACOUSTIC
00699614..$14.99

FINGERPICKING ACOUSTIC CLASSICS
00160211..$14.99

FINGERPICKING ACOUSTIC HITS
00160202..$12.99

FINGERPICKING ACOUSTIC ROCK
00699764..$12.99

FINGERPICKING BALLADS
00699717..$12.99

FINGERPICKING BEATLES
00699049..$19.99

FINGERPICKING BEETHOVEN
00702390..$8.99

FINGERPICKING BLUES
00701277 ....$9.99

FINGERPICKING BROADWAY FAVORITES
00699843..$9.99

FINGERPICKING BROADWAY HITS
00699838..$7.99

FINGERPICKING CELTIC FOLK
00701148..$10.99

FINGERPICKING CHILDREN'S SONGS
00699712..$9.99

FINGERPICKING CHRISTIAN
00701076 ....$7.99

FINGERPICKING CHRISTMAS
00699599..$9.99

FINGERPICKING CHRISTMAS CLASSICS
00701695..$7.99

FINGERPICKING CHRISTMAS SONGS
00171333..$9.99

FINGERPICKING CLASSICAL
00699620..$10.99

FINGERPICKING COUNTRY
00699687..$10.99

FINGERPICKING DISNEY
00699711..$15.99

FINGERPICKING EARLY JAZZ STANDARDS
00276565 ....$12.99

FINGERPICKING DUKE ELLINGTON
00699845..$9.99

FINGERPICKING ENYA
00701161..$10.99

FINGERPICKING FILM SCORE MUSIC
00160143..$12.99

FINGERPICKING GOSPEL
00701059..$9.99

FINGERPICKING GUITAR BIBLE
00691040 ....$19.99

FINGERPICKING HIT SONGS
00160195..$12.99

FINGERPICKING HYMNS
00699688..$9.99

FINGERPICKING IRISH SONGS
00701965..$9.99

FINGERPICKING ITALIAN SONGS
00159778..$12.99

FINGERPICKING JAZZ FAVORITES
00699844..$9.99

FINGERPICKING JAZZ STANDARDS
00699840..$10.99

FINGERPICKING ELTON JOHN
00237495..$12.99

FINGERPICKING LATIN FAVORITES
00699842..$9.99

FINGERPICKING LATIN STANDARDS
00699837..$12.99

FINGERPICKING ANDREW LLOYD WEBBER
00699839..$14.99

FINGERPICKING LOVE SONGS
00699841..$12.99

FINGERPICKING LOVE STANDARDS
00699836 ....$9.99

FINGERPICKING LULLABYES
00701276..$9.99

FINGERPICKING MOVIE MUSIC
00699919..$10.99

FINGERPICKING MOZART
00699794..$9.99

FINGERPICKING POP
00699615..$12.99

FINGERPICKING POPULAR HITS
00139079..$12.99

FINGERPICKING PRAISE
00699714..$10.99

FINGERPICKING ROCK
00699716..$12.99

FINGERPICKING STANDARDS
00699613..$12.99

FINGERPICKING WEDDING
00699637..$9.99

FINGERPICKING WORSHIP
00700554..$10.99

FINGERPICKING NEIL YOUNG – GREATEST HITS
00700134..$14.99

FINGERPICKING YULETIDE
00699654..$9.99

HAL•LEONARD®

Visit Hal Leonard online at www.halleonard.com

Prices, contents and availability
subject to change without notice.